NORTH-WEST BUSES IN THE 1980S

PAUL WILLIAMS

AMBERLEY

First published 2017

Amberley Publishing
The Hill, Stroud
Gloucestershire, GL5 4EP

www.amberley-books.com

Copyright © Paul Williams, 2017

The right of Paul Williams to be identified as
the Author of this work has been asserted in
accordance with the Copyrights, Designs and
Patents Act 1988.

ISBN 978 1 4456 6944 1 (print)
ISBN 978 1 4456 6945 8 (ebook)

British Library Cataloguing in Publication Data.
A catalogue record for this book is available from
the British Library.

Origination by Amberley Publishing.
Printed in the UK.

Contents

Foreword

This book isn't meant as any kind of definitive history: it's the observations and musings of an observer of the North West transport scene through one of its most tumultuous but interesting periods. This was the era of Thatcher, the miners' strike and, above all for these pages, bus deregulation in 1986. The decade probably saw the most change in bus travel for fifty years, with many upheavals; some were undoubtedly good and needed, some were less welcome as competition sometimes overcame common sense.

There is no attempt to cover every single type of bus and every location in the five counties in the scope of this book: it's just not possible and there must be a balance between the commonplace and the unusual. So clutch your Every Bus Saver (Manchester), Red Rose Rambler (Lancashire) or your Saveaway (Merseyside) and enjoy the ride.

Introduction

To understand the present, we need to learn a little about the past. As in so many avenues of innovation, the North West of England was the birthplace of passenger transport. The first public passenger railway was, famously, the Liverpool and Manchester Railway, opened in 1830, but this was already six years after the first public omnibus service in the United Kingdom – a regular service between Pendleton Toll Bar and Manchester – had been started in January 1824 by a certain John Greenwood. Londoners celebrate Shillibeer's Omnibus to the Bank of 1829: but once again what Manchester thinks today, the world thinks tomorrow. Then the very first demonstration of the tram in our country took place in 1860, in Birkenhead; a certain George Francis Train, an American citizen, had seen primitive street tramway systems in the USA and brought the idea to Europe.

So by the end of the nineteenth century, private investors had created horse bus and horse tram networks all over the country, and perhaps at their most comprehensive in the North West – the most industrialised and busiest part of the Kingdom outside London. They were encouraged by the 1870 Tramways Act, which gave the rich new municipal boroughs the power to construct street tramways, but not to operate them – leasing them to companies instead.

But the power of the great municipal cities was rising, and this – together with some shady practices by some of the private lessees to run as few services as possible for as much money as possible – prompted a change in the law to allow the local authorities to operate the trams themselves. This was the city – and the town – in its pomp, and soon 'Liverpool Corporation Tramways' was as familiar on the banks of the Mersey as 'Accrington Corporation' was in the brick-making Mecca.

The end of the Great War brought great change. In particular the motor lorry and by extension the motor bus had evolved in reliability and speed, and what's more the Military was selling off their unwanted lorries to ex-soldiers with their war pensions, many of them starting haulage or bus businesses with them. Some of these were tiny acorns that remained tiny, and failed within a few short years. Others grew into mighty bus companies, usually with backing from the Tilling or British Electric Traction combines – Ribble and North Western both broke much new territory as pioneers using the new buses to open up public transport to places that had only ever seen a pony and trap before.

So the trams faded away, the last in the region being in Liverpool in 1957 – if you ignore the Blackpool operation, run as a tourist attraction as much as a public service. Trolleybuses – buses, but with electric motors and long booms connected to overhead wires – came and went. The first in our region was as far back as 1912 in Stockport, and the last in Manchester and Ashton was in 1966.

By the 1960s it all felt very settled. Cherry-red Ribble buses in most of Lancashire and most of what is now Cumbria; brighter red Lancashire United in the south Lancashire belt; North Western in most of Cheshire and the Peak District; Cumberland in, er, Cumberland; Crosville in south Merseyside, the Wirral and west Cheshire. Almost every town of appreciable size had a municipal bus fleet, from mighty Manchester with over a thousand buses to tiny Ramsbottom, with eleven, but the first of the great upheavals in 1969 would change all that.

The Transport Secretary, Barbara Castle, was very exercised by the problems of city transport and thought that transport in the large conurbations should come under unified control. So on 1 November 1969 the eleven municipal bus operators in and around Manchester were combined into a new SELNEC Passenger Transport Executive (PTE) – thankfully known as SELNEC for short. One month later a similar exercise on the Mersey created Merseyside PTE, combining the Liverpool undertaking with Birkenhead and Wallasey, even though the amount of interworking between them was very limited due to the river.

The new 'normal' in these big cities was orange in Manchester and, after a dalliance with different colours on each side of the river, Verona green on Merseyside. 1974 brought local government reorganisation – a hot topic in town halls the length and breadth of the country – but in North West transport terms the visible change wasn't great; St Helens and Southport joined with Merseyside and Wigan joined Greater Manchester Transport. Lancaster City Transport merged with Morecambe & Heysham, while a few well-loved municipal names were replaced by bland 1970s titles like Halton or Hyndburn.

In the 'territory' companies, the changes were for the most part under the skin. Crosville, Ribble and Cumberland were now National Bus Company subsidiaries and had to choose between NBC Leaf Green and Poppy Red. Crosville chose the former, Ribble and Cumberland chose the latter, making it hard to tell their buses apart in border towns like Millom and Penrith. North Western, sadly, disappeared altogether; SELNEC had made an offer that couldn't be refused to NBC for the North Western services in its area. Deprived of the profitable urban services, what was left wasn't viable and was split between Crosville (Cheshire) and Trent (Derbyshire), bringing Crosville green into surprising new locations like Macclesfield. Lancashire United was bought by Greater Manchester in 1976 but for now was kept separate, still in its red and grey livery.

And so once again we seemed to reach stability in our region – two PTEs, three NBC subsidiaries, and a dozen local authority operators. The buzzword was 'coordination', and the bus operators of the North West knew a thing or two about that, having lived cheek-by-jowl and with many co-ordination agreements reached over many years. So, for example, in 1982 there was a recast of services in Rossendale with joint working by Rossendale Transport, Ribble, Burnley & Pendle and Greater Manchester. In Merseyside the co-ordination was a little more one-sided; MPTE was less than happy about so many services in the south being operated by Crosville and in the north by Ribble, but they were too big to buy.

But just as it all seemed to be reaching maturity, upheaval was again around the corner in the shape of bus deregulation on 26 October 1986. If 1969 affected some parts of our region, 1986 simply took the whole edifice and turned it upside down. GMT became GM Buses, with its optimistic advertising slogan 'Pick you up tomorrow as usual' (with a fleet downsizing of one third overnight, that wasn't necessarily true). Merseyside became Merseybus. The local authorities clung on to their local town operations, although quite a few decided to branch out, such as Blackburn, who decided to fight with Ribble on the express services to Manchester.

The NBC subsidiaries had their own problems: the government had decided to privatise them one by one and, on the way, split the ones that they regarded as too big and powerful. Of course that meant the mighty Ribble and the almost-as-mighty Crosville each split into two. Ribble became Ribble in the north and reused the proud North Western name in west Lancashire and Merseyside; Crosville, logically, split into English and Welsh arms.

On top of this, the new deregulated market was entered – some might say 'swamped' – by new operators. Some were established, like Mayne's of Manchester or Fishwick's of Leyland, others were new to service buses – often coach operators who saw an opportunity. Most were small operations with just a few routes and the majority were soon gone. A few were major entrants, with big money behind them, such as Zippy in Preston and Bee Line in Manchester, and everywhere there were minibuses, cheap to buy and cheap to run as drivers were usually paid less to drive them than full-size vehicles.

If it wasn't a bloodbath, it was certainly unsettling. Co-ordination was out, competition was in. Ribble fought pitched battles with Barrow and Lancaster Boroughs; there could be only one winner of those contests, so Barrow's own local bus company was gone by the end of the decade and Lancaster went in the early 90s. The new independents found life hard, both because the bigger operators were ready and willing to fight, sometimes with borderline tactics such as running just ahead of the competitor, but often because they found that running a reliable bus service, day in day out, isn't easy and not a passport to riches.

By the late eighties, the new normal was that very little was normal. Ribble fought GM Buses on the core 582 Bolton – Leigh route that had once been a trolleybus service; Merseybus fought Fareway and Liverbus tooth and nail; Hyndburn found itself in a struggle with newcomer Pilkington's and Accrington Coachways.

There were unexpected casualties as well as the one-sided David-and-Goliath wars. Long-established Yelloway was under new management and used its much-loved prestige heritage to run the scruffiest, most run-down buses it was possible to find outside a scrapyard. It didn't last long. Crosville lost its way completely, being bought by neighbour Potteries. Cumberland, meanwhile, became the first North West purchase of Stagecoach, with Ribble following soon after – bringing the blue, red, and orange stripes to our region.

There were unexpected success stories too. Mayne has already been mentioned, expanding from one route to a whole network in east Manchester built on a diet of ex-London DMS Fleetlines that London thought were 'rubbish', but which found very gainful employment everywhere else. Companies such as Kirkby Lonsdale Coaches, Aintree Coachlines, and Mountain Goat found their niche often in the less intensively competitive areas and survive to this day.

So overall, the contrast between the North West in 1980 and 1990 couldn't be greater. In 1980, with some exceptions, the bus scene looked quite a lot like that in 1970 or even 1960 – long-established services, little change over the years, peaceful and probably complacent regulation and co-ordination. By 1990 it was all different – competition was king, many new names had arrived on the scene (and quite a few had already gone). You could either regard it as the long-overdue shake-up of a cartel that had become fat and lazy, or you could think of it as a classic case of the baby departing with the bath water and the triumph of capitalism over public service. Either way, the 1980s marked a period of tumultuous change in the North West's buses and this book can only scratch the surface of the transformation.

Cheshire

Cheshire was, and is, a county of more contrast than it is given credit for. Of course it has the leafy lanes of Wilmslow and Goostrey – and Chester itself is generally not short of a bob or two – but it also has industry in Macclesfield and Northwich, and east Cheshire is right up in the Peak District; remember that it's hard to get from Greater Manchester to Derbyshire without crossing into Cheshire first, usually at Whaley Bridge.

In 1980, Cheshire's buses were dominated by Crosville Motor Services. From its headquarters at Crane Wharf, Chester, its green buses permeated almost every corner of the county. In 1972 it had acquired the Cheshire services of North Western, bringing it bases in Northwich, Macclesfield and even Biddulph in Staffordshire. In 1980 it seemed very odd to find one of the last Bristol Lodekkas in Warrington rubbing shoulders in Arpley bus station with Greater Manchester Standards, but around places like Knutsford or Crewe, Crosville Nationals or Bristol REs were standard fare.

In 1980 there were three municipal operators in the county. There was Chester City Transport on Crosville's doorstep; Warrington; and Halton, which had before 1974 been 'Widnes Corporation' and whose buses still mainly stuck to the north side of the birdcage bridge over the Mersey. Independents were few and far between, as it wasn't obviously lucrative bus territory, but they were there all right, including Devaway that was set up by redundant ex-Crosville managers at deregulation and did so well that it outlasted Crosville itself.

Most of Cheshire is hardly a fertile land for intensive bus operation, given its predilection for Range Rovers, but 1986 still brought much change. Parallel to the deregulation of bus services, National Bus Company subsidiaries were privatised and the very biggest, including Crosville, were instructed to divide into smaller units. Crosville chose a rather neat split between its English and Welsh operations, but the new owners of the English side were far from a credit to the bus industry – perhaps their most notable achievement was to buy Yelloway, proud Rochdale coach operator, and kill it in a flurry of public inquiries and broken-down crocks. Crosville soon started to follow in the same direction, and it didn't take long for it to pass through a succession of owners, gradually disappearing as it did so until there was nothing left. Chester City

Transport survived the 1980s, although it too succumbed after the end of the century. Warrington's main threat came from a different direction. The new southern half of Ribble, named North Western in one of the biggest traductions of a proud heritage, decided that Warrington was a target and flooded the town; each fought the other to a standstill until an uneasy stalemate was reached.

Halton survived and actually did reasonably well, probably helped by the internal upheaval of likely competitors Crosville. It expanded north towards Liverpool but made sure to look after its 'home' territory in and around Widnes, building up fierce local loyalty.

By 1989, the county had settled down but not without big changes. Crosville was moving but dying on its feet, and indeed in 1990 the Chester and Wirral operations were sold to Potteries Motor Traction – no doubt to the bemusement of Wirrallers seeing 'Crosville' emblazoned on red buses. Municipal Halton, Chester, and Warrington still survived, and North Western prowled the north part of the county.

Northwich was classic Crosville territory – except it wasn't, as until 1972 it had been North Western's western outpost. By 1980 everything was NBC leaf-green, including Leyland National SNG380 in the town's bus station.

Runcorn's busway was completed in 1977 and was an unguided precursor to more recent systems. Most of it is still in use today but you'll no longer find Crosville SRG64 on it, complete with Busway branding.

I confess I know nothing about Hadyn Jones Coaches of Macclesfield, and I even wonder if the signwriter shouldn't have put 'Haydn' – but there's no doubting the bus; it's a former East Midland Leopard with Weymann body.

After the end of North Western, Crosville was dominant in most of Cheshire and spread its tentacles into neighbouring Staffordshire, with Bristol VR DVG471 leaning into Newcastle-under-Lyme bus station.

Macclesfield was a handsome town, with a handsome ex-North Western bus station and garage, served in 1980 by handsome buses. Crosville SRL236 had started life as North Western 361 but had transferred when only a few months old.

It was still possible to see Bristol Lodekkas in service around Warrington at the start of the 1980s if you were lucky; DFG170 was sixteen years old when photographed but was still good for a couple of gentle school runs each day.

Leyland Nationals weren't everyone's cup of tea but they were more bearable in the dual-purpose configuration, and Crosville had some for inter-urban services. ENL832 had either been, or was about to embark, on a trip between Northwich and the not-inter-urban destination of Moulton.

Chester's buses were 'proper' municipal – corporation maroon and cream, nice clear destination, and some lovely buses. Number 1 was a Guy Arab with Massey body new in 1953 and nominally still in the fleet in the 1980s, but in reality the fleet's 'pet'.

Chester didn't want Nationals and couldn't get single deckers with Gardner engines, so bought Leopards – several with these Northern Counties bodies that were functional rather than pretty. 69 was new in January 1976 and was the first of three.

The Bristol RE was the king of Cheshire – Crosville had hundreds, Warrington liked them, and Halton Borough, based in Widnes, standardised on them for several years in an all-single deck fleet. 5 was typical, with East Lancs body and dual doors.

Like many municipals, Chester always bought new, but after deregulation it dabbled in the second-hand market, acquiring number 12, which had been new to Highland Scottish and sold off early. It lasted all the way to the end of Chester's existence as a separate operator.

Chester tried a special livery for coach and private hire vehicles, and this is the less-than-happy result that appeared only on number 80. The chassis in the background could be that of Fleetline 57, which had been fire-damaged and was eventually given a new body in 1985.

Chester liked Gardner engines; so it was a loyal Daimler Fleetline customer, even after the chassis was made in Leyland. But few Leyland Fleetlines were badged so proudly as 93 on the right, whereas 62 on the left is far too modest to admit its Coventry origins.

35 was a typical later Guy Arab for Chester – Massey body and sliding 'bacon slicer' door. They were solid as a rock and Chester went on to buy the last three Guy Arabs of them all, late enough to be the only ones with an 'H' suffix registration.

After Massey's closed, Chester's custom went to the other end of Wigan in Northern Counties, which later relocated to the old Massey factory anyway. So 90 was very much in the Chester tradition – Gardner-engined chassis and body made in Pemberton.

These Chester Leopards with Duple Dominant bodies were pretty things, but the bodywork structure wasn't too strong and few had very long lives. 73 appears to be advertising Fiat cars, which is ironic as Fiats of this period were also known for being pretty but rusting to death.

Halton Borough Transport moved from Bristol REs to Leyland Nationals, including a very early one, and got very good results out of them – no doubt in a small fleet it was easier to anticipate trouble. 20 was one of three delivered in 1977.

116 was Warrington's trainer in the early 1980s and could often be found hanging round Warrington bus station. The elongated 'W' for the Borough Council symbol was uninspired, and so was the livery – 116 looked better later, when it got its old 'Corporation' livery back.

North Western bought 'special' Bristol REs with low rooflines for its Altrincham – Warrington service via Dunham Massey bridge. Shortly after, the route passed to Crosville and the REs could be found on all Crosville's Warrington routes, but SRL244 was seen in Altrincham on the service for which it was intended.

Warrington bought Atlanteans or Fleetlines, but usually stayed loyal to East Lancs bodywork. 34 was a Fleetline and was seen at the new bus station helping Fred Dibnah sell Greenall's Local Bitter, brewed in Warrington. Awful bus station, awful beer, nice bus.

For single deck services, Warrington dabbled in the Seddon RU but alighted upon the Bristol RE for as long as it could get them. 63 had the inevitable East Lancs Body and was about to embark on the trip to Old Hall west of the town centre, part of the booming 'new town'.

It looks like Warringtonians couldn't take a hint – 21 was pretty insistent on asking only for the exact fare with no change. It was a late Atlantean with the usual East Lancs body, one of three you can see outside the bus station.

Lancashire United had run into Warrington for years, but by the 1980s it was being subsumed by the giant Greater Manchester Transport. Ex-London DMS 2325 was painted orange but carried LUT fleetnames. If you like DMSs that's good, as we will encounter them again.

Halton, unlike their Cheshire municipal neighbours, went for Leyland Nationals and especially National 2s – in fact it took the very last one. 30 was typical but, untypically, spent a couple of weeks when new in Blackpool where it helped influence the purchase of the same type there.

Warrington caught the DMS bug, but at least it had had Fleetlines before. There were six of them, bought in 1980 when seven years old, and they were a bargain. 97 did seven years in the town then went on to Lincoln City Transport before meeting its maker in 1990.

It seemed odd in what had been a Lancashire town, to see Crosville buses darting around. SNL663 was approaching the bus station and was a podless 'Series B' National and a poor replacement for an ex-North Western Bristol RE.

Crosville SRG213 was converted in 1981 to carry wheelchairs, with some high-backed seats arranged longitudinally. It was known as the 'Easy Rider' and lasted a few years then was sold for scrap – what a shame it wasn't donated to an organisation who could've made use of it.

After production of the Fleetline ended and as the Atlantean wound down, Warrington turned to the Dennis Dominator – with East Lancs body, of course. 48 was new when photographed in the bus station in 1983 and after sale went on to new owners in Bagillt and Auchinleck before being scrapped in 2010.

It's deregulation day, 26 October 1986, and a commemorative rally is being held in Chester. Northern Counties displayed the Future of Buses – a minibus, or 'midibus' if you believe the number plate, based on a Dodge chassis. It was indeed the future for a while, as subsequent pages will show.

Not content with buying ex-Derby Fleetlines in 1980, Warrington went back for more – this time, Olympians with East Lancs bodies. Number 39 here even took the number of one of its Derbyshire predecessors. They were often to be found on the 19 to Leigh, set up in competition with GM Buses.

Devaway of Chester was set up by ex-Crosville managers at deregulation and gave Crosville a very good run for their money. Ex-Halton REs were the backbone and this one still carries its Halton number 10. In fact Devaway outlasted Crosville, finally selling out to Arriva Wales in 1998.

Before privatisation, Crosville had developed a 'town lynx' identity for limited-stop services and its post-privatisation livery incorporated the lynx into its fleet name. Sadly for Crosville the company turned out to be less agile than the cat and was gone within a few years of privatisation.

Merseyside

In 1980 Merseyside was regarded by some as the sick man of Britain – it had a reputation for strikes, deprivation, Militant and crime. There's no doubt that these were tough times for Liverpool but it was only half the story: Merseyside was vibrant and determined to see the tough times through.

It was, of course, the home of Merseyside Passenger Transport Executive. MPTE had inherited the municipal undertakings of Liverpool, Wallasey, Birkenhead, Southport and St Helens between 1969 and 1974 – not the most obvious bedfellows, as there had been less interworking between them than over in Greater Manchester. Meanwhile, National Bus Company behemoths Crosville in the south and west, and Ribble in the east and north, loomed over Merseyside and dominated nominally PTE areas such as most of the Wirral (Crosville) and the Bootle/Kirkby area (Ribble). Meanwhile east of St Helens, in Newton-le-Willows, Greater Manchester was the exclusive provider as successor to Lancashire United.

Merseyside's municipal inheritance was disappearing quickly in 1980, with not many pre-1969 buses left. Instead what we had was plenty of Leyland Atlanteans with Alexander or East Lancs bodies in Verona green, cream, and with brown trimmings. They were sturdy and very, very spartan. Of course, they weren't the only thing on offer – there was the usual offering of Leyland Nationals plus, in 1980, if you knew where to look, you might find a batch of Bristol REs with ECW bodies that could have been National Bus Company infiltrators in disguise. There was also a smallish coaching arm and a fairly substantial minority of Bristol VRs with East Lancs or Willowbrook bodies plus some MCW Metropolitans; Merseyside was one of several operators to try them in frustration at Leyland's inability to deliver buses on time.

Crosville had been a Tilling company and it showed. You could still find Lodekkas in 1980, especially on the routes to Warrington and Chester, but within a couple of years they were gone. However, there were swarms of Bristol REs, Bristol VRs, Leyland Nationals in bus and dual purpose versions, and some exotica such as Seddon RUs, from an order of 100, which was the biggest order for the model. You might even find a few interesting second-hand purchases, such as a few ex-Southdown Fleetlines and ex-Sheffield Bristol VRs with East Lancs bodies. Very occasionally, you might even see a Bristol SC4LK single-deck rural bus escape from some Welsh outstation and get as far as Pier Head.

Ribble had been a BET company. On Merseyside in 1980 its thing was full-front PDs, Atlanteans, and Bristol REs – for some reason, although their Leyland Nationals weren't unknown on Merseyside, they weren't quite as common on this part of their patch as in other parts of Ribble territory.

Merseyside PTE and their political masters weren't happy about huge swathes of their county being served by NBC subsidiaries, but they were too big to buy or force out, so the weapon of choice was PTE subsidiary or lack thereof. Merseyside was proud of its electric rail system and the PTE was generally quite rail-minded, so the buzz phrase was road-rail co-ordination with enforced interchanges at places like Waterloo, with as many Ribble (in this case) or Crosville services as possible forced to terminate at Merseyrail stations instead of in the city centre. At deregulation they were shown up to be the white elephants they were, as buses ignored them and swept past to take part in the maelstrom that was Liverpool city centre in 1986.

Deregulation hit Liverpool hard. Ribble's southern area became North Western and used their bases in the area to target the northern half of Merseyside, but the storm in the city centre came from a crop of new operators – Fareway, Liverline, Merseyline, and Liverbus to name but a few. It wasn't sustainable and consolidation took place at dizzying speed in the following decade, but the late 80s for Merseyside were colourful, chaotic, and competitive.

A Verona green and cream Atlantean on the 79 from Netherley – this must be Liverpool Pier Head, and it is, but the blue 'Catherine wheel' says it's a Wirral division bus, so presumably it was on loan to cover a shortage.

Crosville found itself a few buses short in the early eighties so went on a buying spree. HDG900 was an ex-Southdown Fleetline, so at least it had a Gardner engine. But if the upstairs windscreen ever broke, it's unlikely the storesman would be able to offer another one.

Merseyside 1651 was an Edge Lane bus so would have trod the path of the 40 to Litherland many times. It looked as though it could have done with a visit to the works next door as it was looking a bit shabby when photographed at Pier Head in August 1985.

Merseyside also bought a few Atlanteans with East Lancs bodies, including 1706 seen at Pier Head bus station. They were very spartan and built to a price, and you can hear the rivets rattling just looking at her.

Crosville's second-hand purchases from Southdown included HDL922. This time the storesman would be happier with an ECW body, but the 'L' in the fleet number tells us that it's one of a minority of Fleetlines built with Leyland engines.

The third Crosville second-hander was probably closest to the ideal of what was available. It's ex-Sheffield Corporation, and East Lancs body, neither obvious choices – but despite appearances it was a Bristol VR, and on the body at least all the glass was flat.

Up the coast from Liverpool is Southport, placed within Merseyside but not really happy about it. Perhaps in recognition, Southport's MPTE divisional colour was Southport Corporation red – and the ex-Corpy open toppers were proudly kept in full Southport livery complete with lining-out.

More mundane ex-Southport buses had to make do in Verona green. 89 fitted in well to a Merseyside fleet full of Alexander-bodied Atlanteans but in fact it had been new to the Corporation in red and cream. It had a second life as a caravan and is thought to still exist in preservation.

Southport had its portion of standard MPTE Atlanteans too, but they always somehow seemed a little out-of-place like a gritty, no-nonsense stranger in a genteel town. 1728 ended up in Manchester working for MTL Manchester, the tit-for-tat competitor at war with GM Buses.

This was more like it for Southport residents, a nice comfy Leopard with a Duple body and coach seats. Merseyside 7003 was being used on the town park and ride next to the War Memorial and I'd have swapped my Ford Sierra for a ride on this any day.

Of course the 'other' bus operator in Southport was Ribble, which had a grand bus station (converted from a railway station) but whose buses were banned from Lord Street until deregulation by arcane licensing agreements. 774 was pretty typical local fare when photographed in July 1982.

Merseyside also had Nationals, with quite a few at St Helens taking over from life-expired Swifts. The 1 was the PTE's single route that went far into Greater Manchester, successor to an old trolleybus service that had been joint between St Helens Corporation and Lancashire United.

When the Atlantean's production run was ending, MPTE tried offerings from several suppliers. This included a pair of Volvo B55s including 0054 here. As deregulation approached, the pace of new buys slowed down and there was never a new generation of standardised buses as had been seen with the Atlantean.

Brockhouse Maxwell attempted to break into the bus gearbox business and adapted an old DMS as a test bed and demonstrator. Merseyside tried it for a few weeks in 1984 and numbered it 8000, but severe teething problems were never overcome.

National 2s were good buses – solid bodies, and no more dreadful 500-series engines. St Helens took well to their allocation and shortly after taking this picture, the photographer was treated to an exhilarating run up Haresfinch Road in the direction of Billinge.

Ormskirk is in Lancashire of course, but it had a Merseyside 'feel' with green MPTE and red Ribble buses available. These ECW-bodied Atlanteans could be found in most corners of the Ribble empire but Merseyside had a lot of them, including 1406.

Ten of these little Dennis Lancets arrived in 1983 and they could be found doing odd jobs in the outer reaches of Merseyside. 7021 was in St Helens operating the infrequent 99 to Kings Moss, right on the fringe of the county near Billinge.

Liverpool city centre wasn't the obvious place for an open-topper but Ribble's 1927 was on a blood donation drive there in August 1985. It was new to Devon General and survives in preservation today back in Devon General livery.

There was a corner of Merseyside that never saw green buses for most of the existence of Merseyside county – Newton-le-Willows, which had been Lancashire United territory. GMT 6982 was on a former LUT service in August 1985 and was a Fleetline with Northern Counties body.

When Ribble was split up just before deregulation, the 'south' division was split off and given an illustrious name – North Western. The livery was less prestigious but when first applied it could look quite smart although the depot's bill for masking tape probably went up a lot.

At deregulation, Merseyside PTE's buses became Merseybus but still in Verona green and cream. 1692 was at Pier Head but both it and the Pier Head bus station's days were numbered – the Pier Head bus station was demolished in 1990 while 1692 went for scrap a year later.

Deregulation brought competition to Liverpool in a big way. Fareway was first out of the gate, formed by four ex-MPTE staff made redundant, with ex-London DMS buses at the heart of the start-up as in so many other places. Its base was in Kirkby and its low fares were very popular at a time of economic hardship.

Merseyside bought thirty Atlanteans with Willowbrook bodies including 1848, seen at Pier Head. They weren't MPTE's best – Willowbrook had a poor reputation and they were withdrawn at a young age while older Alexanders were kept. This one saw further service with G and G of Leamington Spa but it was out of use by the mid-90s.

At first, the only difference between MPTE and Merseybus livery was the fleet name, and 6143 looked very similar in 1989 to how it did in 1985. It was photographed in Hall Street, St Helens, across the road from the old garage that had by now become a bus museum.

Merseyside PTE buses became Merseybus, so the coaches became… Merseycoach. 7019 was a fair way from its home when it visited Showbus at Woburn Abbey in 1988 – at the time this event was nicknamed 'Showerbus' due to its uncanny ability to attract rain each year.

Merseybus decided to break from its PTE image and the surprising result was a very traditional crimson and cream scheme that was very attractive. 1666 did a good job of brightening up Pier Head bus station on a murky day in July 1989.

Liverline was another independent that sprang up at deregulation. Whereas Fareway ran north towards Kirkby, Liverline could be found in the Speke and Halewood areas. After a couple of years it sold out to North Western's owner Drawlane, but this ex-Glasgow Atlantean didn't run for the new owner.

Crosville's Rock Ferry depot was the base of DOG125, seen competing with a Merseybus Olympian. It all looks quite serene but all was not well with Crosville and the company was eventually broken up piecemeal – with a last rump of depots at Rock Ferry and Chester being sold to Potteries Motor Traction, of all people.

Merseyside PTE had always been quite rail-orientated and would never have contemplated a Liverpool – Southport bus service, but North Western had no such qualms and ex-Ribble 407 was doing duty on the 300 when photographed, right outside Southport railway station.

Merseyside PTE bought penny numbers of Dennis Dominators now and again, fifteen in total, perhaps to keep Leyland on their toes. 0035 was one of just a pair, and arrived in 1982. We see it later in the decade at the Roe Street stops, and with a terrible early dot-matrix display.

In 1989 Aintree Coachline were looking for a Dominator for local hire and schools work. Instead they found themselves the owner of TUB250R, the ex-West Yorkshire Foden-NC that was just one of seven completed. They still own and cherish it today.

This is the first time in these pages we have seen an ex-GM Standard bus sold after deregulation, but it is far from the last. Fareway built up a fleet of these as it grew, and it competed strongly against Merseybus before selling to its competitor in 1992.

Liverbus of Huyton was another post-dereg competitor and again built its fleet in GM Standards. Fareway preferred Fleetlines but Liverbus liked Atlanteans, including this one which had been new to Greater Manchester as their 7658.

Typical
post-deregulation
Merseyside – Liverline
34 is pursued by two
Merseybus Atlanteans,
with the maroon
one also heading to
Halewood. 34 was
new to Plymouth City
Transport.

Merseyside came
late to the Metrobus
party – they only
bought them in penny
numbers before
deregulation, but then
as Merseybus took a
further twenty-five
in 1989. 0057 was
rare in being an
Alexander-bodied
Metrobus and was to
be found at Belle Vale
in January 1988.

Aintree-based CMT
was new to stage
carriage services but it
wasn't a new business,
having been a coach
operator for many
years. It specialised in
tendered Merseytravel
services including
'Mobility bus' services,
which is how we
see ex-Southdown
National UFG47S
with a wheelchair-lift
just ahead of the
rear wheel.

Merseyside loved
its Atlanteans but
eventually knew it
could buy no more.
Even before the last
Atlanteans arrived,
small numbers
of new types
were bought for
evaluation including
five ECW-bodied
Olympians
including 0034.
More Olympians
came later, but not
with ECW bodies.

Well, this was just
taking the mickey,
wasn't it? Ogdens
of St Helens chose
this livery for their
entry to deregulated
bus services, and by
'sheer coincidence'
chose this style
that just happened
to be a copy of
North Western's.
OAH553M had
been new to Eastern
Counties.

Merseybus crimson
was an attractive
livery and perhaps
no type wore it
better than the
National 2s, which
looked classy and
purposeful. 6157
was based in St
Helens and was seen
on a private hire in
October 1989.

Greater Manchester

In 1980, there was just one dominant player in Manchester – Greater Manchester Transport, whose orange buses reached to virtually every corner of the most powerful of the metropolitan counties. GMT's orange buses numbered nearly 3,000, and – at the start of the decade – still contained buses from each of the constituent operators that had joined SELNEC and then Greater Manchester between 1969 and 1976. So despite the influx of hundreds of 'Standard' Atlanteans and Fleetlines, there was still plenty of variety to be seen, especially at the peak hours when everything that was roadworthy was turned out.

Because SELNEC had bought the North Western operations in its area, the National Bus Company's subsidiaries were – National Express services to Manchester apart – confined mainly to the edges of the area. Ribble had garages in Bolton and Wigan, but they supported services running mainly from there to outside the area, rather than inwards towards the regional hub. Crosville's former North Western services brought leaf-green buses into Stockport and Altrincham, and even into Manchester, where former North Western buses still ran on the former North Western services to Macclesfield and the like.

The other splash of colour in a sea of orange was A. Mayne & Son of Clayton, east of the city, who had managed to retain a road service licence in the upheaval of the 1930s and had kept running from Stevenson Square along Ashton New Road ever since. For a long time buses were crimson and duck-egg blue while coaches were red and cream, but by 1980 the buses were becoming red and cream also.

Manchester was a big, busy city, so it's no surprise that at deregulation there was much change. GMT became GM Buses, at first using a local identity for each depot, which for example meant forcing the name 'Atherleigh' on Atherton depot's buses. The new North Western used its Bolton and Wigan bases to compete strongly in the west and north, while Trent and Crosville attacked from the south. Independent operators sprang up everywhere; most were small and unlikely to ever last or to grow, although the more reliable companies such as Jim Stones in Leigh and Stott's of Oldham soon carved out respect and an ongoing business. But the new and big independent in town was Bee Line Buzz, owned and backed by the same BET conglomerate that had once owned North Western and Ribble. Bee Line started with a large fleet of minibuses in the south of Greater Manchester, competing aggressively. GM Buses responded with its fleet of 'Little Gem' minibuses and soon the 'breadvan revolution' was in full swing.

It couldn't last. Competition created innovation and drove down fares in the short term, but the competitors were bleeding each other to death despite minibus drivers earning less than their colleagues on full-size buses. New services that were successful soon outgrew minibuses, while those that were not didn't cover their costs. Soon Bee Line were operating second-hand full size buses and became 'just another bus company' before selling out to the owner of North Western.

For the enthusiast, perhaps the most interesting newcomer was Citibus. This Middleton independent ran an eccentric fleet that at one time or another included ex-Preston Panthers, an ex-Yarmouth Swift, Atlanteans from all over including GMT, at least one Metro-Scania... It was quite a pastime working out what would appear next. They were still there at the end of our review period, but in the early 1990s at last sold out to GM Buses (North). They weren't the only independent, far from it – Wall's of Fallowfield, Stuart's of Hyde, Fingland's of Manchester and of course Mayne's all carved out business for themselves in the 1980s.

It was fascinating, but it was messy. What had been a reasonably well-integrated system in 1986 became, overnight, fragmented and confusing, with sixty-three bus operators in Greater Manchester in 1989. GMPTE, shorn of its bus operating arm, concentrated on helping the public to make sense of it all and dreaming of a Light Rail system that some bright spark had termed 'Metrolink'. Arguably bus use in Greater Manchester (and Merseyside) has never recovered since 1986. There's little doubt that fat, complacent GMT needed reform – but the Transport Act 1985 provided a cure that was perhaps worse than the malady.

SELNEC introduced orange as the primary bus colour in Manchester in 1969 and it had been the main colour for the county's buses ever since. The 1981 incarnation had more orange, less white, and a brown skirt. 8151 was based at Frederick Road in Salford and was photographed in Prestwich.

It's easy to imagine that GMT had a monopoly but it didn't, with quite a strong Ribble network on the northern and western edges plus express routes into Manchester. Leopard 1136 had come from Clitheroe and was on its way to Chorlton St coach station.

GMT had a big fleet of Nationals, but 236 was unusual in that it had been new to Lancashire United as its 551. The 673 service was also ex-LUT and 236 had just done the service's Park Lane diversion – which as one of the wealthiest areas of Greater Manchester probably didn't create much custom.

Ah, a proper Lancashire United bus! 432 was one of just a couple of short PSU4 Leopards bought just as LUT became part of Greater Manchester Transport. Although LUT was absorbed in 1981, in June 1983 432 was still in red and grey as it visited Whitefield bus station.

GMT bought nearly 200 Metrobuses, which tended to be used at the Manchester and eastern area depots. 5140 was based at Queens Road and had just left Manchester Arndale bus station, which could most charitably be described as 'dingy'.

National Travel West was based at the old North Western depot in Hulme Hall Road, Manchester. 99 was one of two experimental Dennis Falcons with impressive Duple 'Goldliner' bodywork. They looked the business but they were appalling in every way and 99 didn't even last four years before being scrapped.

Lancashire United had bought Bristol REs by the dozen, mainly with Plaxton bodies, and the last few received the later GMT colour scheme. They looked a lot better in red as we can tell from this shot of 422 in Earlestown over the border in Merseyside.

Meanwhile to the west in Wigan, NBC poppy red was common as Ribble had a depot there and ran services north to Chorley or Preston as well as westwards to Skelmersdale or Southport. 769 had just arrived from Chorley when seen in Wigan Market Place in April 1986.

Greater Manchester kept the Lancashire United identity on coaches even after the buses were repainted orange, using this fetching 'Starsky and Hutch' colour scheme. 615 was one of the last, and was pictured in Atherton garage in April 1984.

Chorlton Street coach station in Manchester was a Mecca for all things National Express, including this Crosville Bristol RE in 'Town Lynx' livery in September 1985. Its sound effects would be wonderful echoing off the walls but the smoke makes me think the injectors needed looking at.

Manchester's gap between the railway stations at Victoria and Piccadilly was filled by Centreline, little buses buzzing through the city at frequent intervals. The first fleet was Seddons but in 1986 they were replaced by Dennis Dominos like 1760 here, which was loaned for a weekend to the Museum of Transport.

At deregulation, Greater Manchester Transport became GM Buses and still in the same livery. Hundreds of older buses were sold off but one that stayed was former GMT 82, which itself was a Duple rebody of a 1975 Leyland Leopard. It carried its age well when seen in Stockport bus station.

Ribble's Wigan depot passed to North Western in 1986, as did former Ribble 1309, which became NW 406 in the company's eccentric colour scheme. These Atlanteans were nicer to ride in than the ECW equivalents and could be found mainly from Preston southwards in Ribble days.

In 1986, the big buzz on the streets of Manchester was the Bee Line Buzz Company. Backed by North Western's former owner BET plc, it launched in great style at deregulation with hordes of minibuses on Ford or Sherpa chassis across the south of Greater Manchester, giving GM Buses much indigestion for a while.

GM Buses' response to the minibus threat was its own fleet, branded 'Little Gem'. Little Gems came as Iveco, Dodge, and as here in Altrincham bus station, MCW Metroriders. The Metroriders were the nicest to ride on but they rotted something chronic and their reputation contributed to the closure of MCW.

Yelloway was a proud name, synonymous with luxurious coach travel, so the tragedy was all the greater when the owner retired and new management dragged the operation and its reputation into the gutter. To say that by 1987 the vehicles shown here represented the cream of the fleet says it all.

Eccles Grey buses were grey, and they were based in Eccles. They were one of a number of 'micro-independents', running just one or two services almost under the radar of the bigger fish. Like many they had some minibuses but, unlike most, they owned a couple of Talbot six wheelers like F249HDB, seen in Cannon Street.

Stott's of Oldham was a case of an old-established coaching company getting into a niche bus operation, being successful by sticking to the local territory and not over-reaching. Like so many it started out with ex-GM Standards like WWH58L, which had once been GMT 7293.

Greater Manchester had bought a couple of hundred Olympians in the early 1980s and they were the backbone of GM Buses for the first few years. 3182 was seen in Leigh but was a Wigan bus, and carried the early 'west area' green strip between the wheelarches.

Wall's of Fallowfield earned a reputation as having a very smart fleet of buses – starting with the inevitable Standards – but made a point of buying some new DAFs with single or double deck bodies. They lasted until 1997, defeated by intense competition on the Wilmslow Road corridor.

For a couple of years after deregulation you literally had no idea what might turn up at the bus stop, especially as operators bid crazy prices for services tendered by Greater Manchester PTE. So the sight of a Crosville Metrorider in Bury Interchange shouldn't have been a surprise, although in truth it was.

Shearing's was part of the mighty Blundell Group with extensive coach operations, so it seemed a logical step when they had a go at local bus services using a mix of second-hand purchases and some new, rather stylish Leyland Tigers with Alexander (Belfast) bodies.

The most common 'Little Gem' type was the Dodge S56 with Northern Counties body like 1943 based at Atherton. Drivers hated them partly because they were horrible and partly because they were allocated to 'low cost units' paying drivers a lower wage than those driving full-size buses.

PRR124L was new to Trent but by 1987 it was one of Yelloway's motley collection, in this case unusually wearing the traditional gold fleetname rather than the modern one on the advert upstairs. Buses came into and out of the Yelloway fleet at such bewildering speed it was hard to keep up.

Crosville didn't so much close as fade away. One of the consequences was SNL668 at Altrincham Interchange, in Crosville livery but North Western fleetnames. It was hardly an advert for public transport and all that can be said about the cleaning of the door is 'try harder next time'.

Unlike all the other independents in Manchester after September 1986, A. Mayne & Son of Clayton had been around for a while – running the only independent service in the city right through Corporation and GMT days. This Fleetline had been new to Mayne's in 1976 and had spent its whole life in the city.

Shearing's bought second-hand as well as new and their number 3 had been Ribble 883 before passing to Cumberland and then Shearing's where it was seen roaring through Albert Square in April 1988, on a spot where now Metrolink trams dominate.

Citibus were, shall we say, a little eccentric in their vehicle purchases. Yes they had GM Standards, but they had a soft spot for Leyland Panthers and other exotica, including RTF436L whose claim to fame was that it was the very last Panther when new to Preston in 1972.

1472 and 1473 were a pair of Dennis Falcons that were based in Leigh and were lightning fast, even if they were unreliable. They gave me many a speedy ride on the 26 from Manchester Arndale bus station on the last evening departure.

Bee Line started to buy bigger buses. 1618 had been new to Southdown but now it was at Manchester's Hulme Hall Road, sharing a garage with North Western as common owner Drawlane streamlined and then merged the two operations.

Mayne's did well, taking care to not stray far from its east Manchester heartland, and so expanded using ex-London DMSs and ex-GM Standards. This had been Greater Manchester 7289 based in Rochdale, but it had been withdrawn at dereg and found itself just down the road in Mayne's garage on Ashton New Road.

Greater Manchester ordered semi-coach double decker bodies from Northern Counties for mounting on Leyland Olympian and MCW Metrobus chassis. This is one of the Metrobuses, leaving Manchester's Piccadilly on the limited stop run to Norden near Rochdale.

North Western's number 1 was a Mercedes mini with conversion by Reeve Burgess. The batch had been ordered by Ribble but North Western had been split off by the time they arrived and 1, with nice seats, was based in Wigan.

The Lancashire United Leopards were long-lived and sturdy, despite having timber-framed bodies. 438 looked smart in Leigh town centre and it's pleasing to note that it's one of two of this class that still exist today in preservation.

Tenders could be won or lost easily so there was much moving around of buses depending on the feast or famine. When Bee Line won extra work, owner Drawlane shipped in some ex-GM Standards from London Country (South West). It wasn't a great advert for the company and the yellow front looked like a British Rail 'warning' panel.

This could be a National Travel garage, but it isn't – it's Yelloway's in Weir Street, Rochdale. Latest addition to the merry-go-round to get a few buses on the road is ex-Ribble 1031, still carrying its former owner's name. It was all to no avail; the Ministry of Transport put an end to this dangerous nonsense in 1988.

Greater Manchester Transport had an extensive training fleet using buses in a distinctive white and yellow livery. Two were dumped at the side of Atherton garage in February 1987, both early Standards. 7227 was a dual-entrance Fleetline, while 7076 was an Atlantean that had been at Bolton when new.

Jim Stones was at the opposite end to Yelloway: modern buses, immaculately kept at their base in Leigh. Jim buys his buses new, but A499MHG was an exception; as a Leyland-DAB Tiger Cub it was a demonstrator but Jim kept it cherished it as a 'pet' and still owns it at the time of writing.

North Western's 723 was an odd addition – it was an impressive MCW Metroliner that had been new to Shamrock & Rambler in Bournemouth. It was used on express services briefly and, converted to open top, later worked until 2013 as a London sightseeing bus.

I've no idea what a Stuart's of Hyde bus was doing on the 32 between Manchester and Wigan – probably a short-lived tender contract. But the photo is here to show the GMPTE 'Every Bus Saver', a post-deregulation Saver Seven, advertised on several fleets in an approximation of the relevant operator's house colours.

By the end of the 1980s Stagecoach branding was coming to Greater Manchester – from the north, in the form of Ribble and its new owners. Ribble 2156 was leaving Bury on a Skipton – Manchester express service that had started before the Second World War and still runs to this day.

The GM Buses 'Little Gem' Ivecos with Robin Hood bodies were the least successful and did not last long. 1542 was dumped at the back of Charles Street for a while, gradually used as a Christmas tree to keep others on the road.

GMT had a successful tours operation known as Charterplan, and the brand was too good to lose after deregulation. Their base was Stockport's Charles Street and it continued to do reasonably well, until the business was sold in the 1990s to East Yorkshire. Number 12 was a Leyland Tiger with Duple 320 body.

One Manchester bright spot in the 1980s was the new Museum of Transport, in Boyle Street outside the city centre. One of its exhibits was – and is – Leigh Corporation 15, and in May 1989 it made a return visit to Leigh bus station to the surprise of the driver of GM Buses 6978 sweeping in at the end of its journey from Manchester.

Lancashire

Lancashire was dominated and varied at the same time. Dominated by Ribble, but with a proud municipal seemingly just over every hill, Lancashire was in 1980 still the home of mighty Leyland whose buses permeated every corner of the red rose county. Ribble was of course a National Bus Company subsidiary, and (in the Frenchwood Avenue HQ) regarded as NBC's jewel in the crown. Ribble was monolithic, it was unbelievably bureaucratic, but it was beloved of enthusiasts everywhere. In 1980 its last Leyland PD3s could be found down in Merseyside and around Preston, while Leyland Leopards and Nationals were everywhere alongside legions of Atlanteans.

Ribble tended to look after the longer inter-urban routes in most places, although there were plenty of exceptions that proved the rule, such as a little network of local services in Fleetwood. Most Lancashire towns still had their own municipal bus fleets who looked after most shorter runs (and some surprisingly longer ones, especially after 1986).

These Lancashire Municipals gave character to almost every medium-sized town in the county: there was Blackpool, in 1980 the home of AEC Swifts, Leyland PD3s, and trams; Fylde next door seemed consciously genteel in comparison with its neighbour, with a conventional but very smart fleet; Preston, with some very odd service numbering quirks, and its brutalist bus station (Ribble services all along one side, Corporation ones on the other). There was Hyndburn, which of course was Accrington with a posh Sunday name, with Atlanteans and Bristol REs in their dark blue and red; Burnley & Pendle, maroon and cream: but GM Roy Marshall allowed himself one little indulgence, which was to paint the coach fleet in biscuit and brown, the traditional livery of East Midland, his local operator in childhood; and Lancaster, an amalgamation of Lancaster and Morecambe & Heysham in 1974, in blue and white distinguishing them from 'enemy' Ribble red.

They all had quirks, but they all had character and they were closely connected with their owners – the towns they served and their ratepayers. But it wasn't enough to save some of them. Almost as soon as deregulation had arrived, Barrow was an early casualty before the 1980s were out, run off the road by competition from Ribble.

Looking forward to the 1990s Lancaster and Hyndburn followed, and in 2016 Lancashire municipally owned bus companies were down to two – Blackpool, who swallowed neighbour Fylde in 1994, and Rossendale, trading under the moronic name 'Rosso'.

Although it wasn't the same chaotic free-for-all as in Manchester or Liverpool, Lancashire still had more than a few new independent operators looking for a slice of the pie; notably but not only in East Lancashire. There was Accrington Coachways, Border of Burnley, and Aspdens of Blackburn, and in the county town the same BET group that brought Bee Line Buzz minibuses to Manchester gave 'Zippy' to Preston. There was less traffic on offer than in the regional capital of course, and two dominant operators (Ribble and Preston) rather than a fragmented market, so it wasn't a huge surprise that Zippy was quickly zipped up and sold to rival Ribble. Other independents and representatives of bigger groups persisted, and there were also operators from over the border in Yorkshire that served the east of the county – Pennine of Gargrave and Keighley & District (successors to the old West Yorkshire Road Car Company) as just two examples.

By 1990 Ribble was Stagecoach Ribble, and the once-proud Frenchwood Avenue bureaucracy was slain. The Borough Councils had adapted to the new world in one or both of two ways – retrenchment and a focus on cutting costs (and no new buses), or trying new markets either for their own sake or to deter the prowling Ribble.

Blackburn and Darwen Corporations had merged in 1974, and to keep all the councillors happy the new livery was an unhappy compromise of Blackburn green and Darwen red. It's a good job 157 was a handsome Tiger Cub with East Lancs body made in the town.

Ribble's home was in Lancashire of course, and their buses could be found in every corner of the county – including Preston, where the HQ and main works was situated and where Bristol RE 334 was found turning into Selborne Street in 1985. There's still a grocer's shop on that corner to this day.

Rawtenstall Corporation Motors had become Rossendale JTC by 1980, but in fact this Leyland PD2 trainer had been new to Haslingden Corporation in their blue and primrose colours. It still survives in preservation but don't go looking for the depot entrance – it's the site of a supermarket now.

Blackpool was famous for pre-war trams... and Leyland PDs, which saw service all day well into the 1980s. 515 was a late one from 1967 and wears the later livery with more green. After sale it got greener still, as a trainer with London and Country whose colours were all-over two-tone green.

Lancaster City Transport was a small operator that, in pre-dereg days, ran a smart and even elegant fleet. This 33-foot Atlantean was typical, and also typical in advertising Mitchell's beer, brewed in the city. 212 ended its days at Travel De Courcey, Warwickshire.

Burnley & Pendle weren't above the odd judicious second-hand purchase but even so, it was still a surprise when some ex-Sunderland Bristol REs came this way complete with avant-garde Strachans bodies. 96 had been Sunderland 102 then Tyneside PTE 1902.

J. Fishwick & Sons was a very long-established independent based in Leyland, and was in some ways Leyland's 'pet' operator with many prototypes and demonstrators coming their way from down the road. But 22 was a very normal East Lancs-bodied Atlantean, almost municipal in design.

Blackburn Borough painted an Atlantean in old-style Blackburn Corporation livery and realised what everyone knew: that it looked far better than the awful red, white, and green. So the whole fleet was painted thus, and looked well for it. 29 was a very late Atlantean with the usual East Lancs body.

Blackpool's tram fleet was mainly made up of pre-war railcoaches and balloons, but some railcoaches were rebuilt with front entrances for one-person operation. To mark the difference they were painted red and cream or yellow like number 13 here, but it's doubtful many people understood the distinction.

Like St Helens, Blackpool liked their AEC Swifts and seemed to get results from them that London couldn't. The seaside town took over fifty, and 574 was from the last batch. The photo was taken by the side of the dingy Talbot Road bus station.

Fylde was the new name for Lytham St Anne's, and their small fleet was regarded as a 'cut above' their brash neighbour. 40 was a Bristol RESL that wouldn't have looked out of place in the Ribble fleet, complete with Preston 'RN' registration, but it was new to the town in 1975.

Chorley depot had a couple of dozen buses and was a friendly place. Ribble 385 was caught there snoozing outside the depot one late afternoon in 1984 after a trip from Preston on the 109.

Blackpool's 'Balloon' trams dated from the 1930s and were imposing beasts, with reversible seats and distinctive art deco interiors. In the 1980s most were still in very close to original condition such as 720 photographed at Manchester Square.

Burnley & Pendle went back to the North East for more second-hand purchases when it bought ten Nationals from Tyne & Wear PTE in 1979. 20 was the first and was a bargain – Burnley got more years out of it than Tyne & Wear did.

Burnley & Pendle Manager Roy Marshall was an enthusiast and fondly recalled his childhood amongst East Midland buses in Nottinghamshire, so when a new livery for B&P coaches was required, 14 and its fellows were given accurate renditions of the old company's livery.

Abbott's of Blackpool ran AECs that were generally Plaxton-bodied, ancient and immaculately presented. OFV467G was sixteen years old when photographed in August 1985 but it was spotless with not a trace of smoke from the exhaust.

For a rural service around the Forest of Bowland, Ribble bought a couple of little Bristol LHs with narrow, short bodies. The route was branded 'Betty's Bus' and that is indeed Mrs Betty Gray, regular driver, at the terminus in Clitheroe.

Rossendale came late to the Atlantean after buying single deckers for most of the 1970s. When they at last arrived they were of course East Lancs-bodied Atlanteans and 26 had been disfigured with an overall advert when photographed in September 1983.

Hyndburn had been Atlantean buyers through the 1970s once Leyland PDs and Guy Arabs went out of production. Their unusual blue and red livery was effective if perhaps a little sombre, and 186 could've benefited from a wash when seen in Blackburn.

RTF561L was unique – it was a prototype for a new National Express fleet. New as Ribble 701 it was an impressive sight. By 1985 it was on hard times and I don't know why it was parked outside Ribble's Frenchwood works, but was on a long series of further owners before expiring for good one day on the M5.

If the East Lancs-bodied Atlantean was the archetypal Lancashire double decker in the 1970s, then the single deck equivalent was the East Lancs-bodied Bristol RE. Rossendale 10 showed off the purposeful lines of the type to good effect when captured in Rawtenstall bus station.

Burnley & Pendle bought Bristol VRs both new and second hand: the first batch included 158, new in 1976 and wearing a pseudo-Burnley Corporation Tramways livery when caught in the town's bus station.

Ribble moved seamlessly from the Atlantean to the Olympian, including taking one of the prototypes. 2122 came from the first batch and was allocated to Burnley who put it to work in October 1985 on the joint 473 via Rawtenstall to Bury.

Fishwick's could usually be relied on to turn out something 'different' and it didn't get much more different than BCK706R, one of the prototype Leyland Titans. This one had done demonstrator work in London and Liverpool before finding its permanent home. It's still preserved today.

Blackpool didn't buy Atlanteans until 1977, and when they did they carried the inevitable East Lancs bodies in this attractive green and cream. 309 was just turning from Lytham Road onto the Promenade when photographed in August 1983.

Ribble's Bristol VRs made a fine sight when freshly painted as 2027 was here. It was posing outside Frenchwood depot in Preston, the company's home and site of its behemoth of a head office. Pity no one thought to touch up the wheels.

Lancaster's stylish Alexander Y-type Leopards were comfortable machines for a small municipal operator, with high-backed seats and a racy 'express' livery. Dusk was falling at Lancaster bus station as 18 rested next to a 'short window' version.

Everyone has an opinion on Preston bus station's architecture but there's no denying it's big. Preston Corporation used one side, Ribble the other. This is clearly the Corporation side and it's post-deregulation – the minibus with 'Preston Buses' on the rear was a new phenomenon.

Blue sky, blue bus and an even more blue bus – after 1986 Fylde had to contend with both Ribble and Blackpool on their doorstep and bought new buses to help compete including the ex-Hull Atlantean on the right. Two-tone blue helped to differentiate with competitors' fleets.

Money for new buses after deregulation was hard to come by, especially full-size buses, so Preston's 1989 Leyland Lynxes were a nice exception. The Lynx acquired a reputation for rusting but that probably didn't worry 211's next owner – it was exported to Malta.

Rossendale expanded quickly at deregulation and one of its more eccentric purchases was this Leopard that had started life as Lancashire United 430. It was a handsome machine but sadly its life in the valley was cut short by accident damage on Rochdale Road in 1988.

Blackpool caught the Routemaster bug, although at least they were a successor of sorts to the town's PD3s. They were given a variation on the old Blackpool Corporation livery and were an alternative to the trams along the Prom for a few years.

Preston liked dual-door buses and 168 is typical as it heads out of the town towards Fulwood. The design of the East Lancs body was such that to fit a side blind, the whole of the first side window downstairs had to be lower, giving this side of the bus a lopsided look.

Ribble's double deck Timesaver livery had blue and red iterations, and this is the red one as seen in Burnley bus station as 2159 embarked on the run to Preston. The inside was fairly standard except for dual-purpose seats, which were all right, but not as good as a GM Buses equivalent.

Lonsdale Coaches of Morecambe had a contract to transport construction workers for the Heysham nuclear power station and could be relied on to have something interesting in the yard. This was once London DM1712 but in June 1985 it had just been bought after a spell in Norwich.

The one-man cars in Blackpool simply wore out, so they were replaced by the 'Centenary' class bodied by East Lancs who, judging by the signs on the pantograph mount, were very proud of the fact. Ten were planned but 641 was the first of just seven after the money ran out.

Burnley & Pendle were perhaps the most surprising Routemaster operator. On acquisition they ran in tatty London red but they were then given smart repaints and an 'East Enders' theme. This one was named *Dirty Den*, which one hopes wasn't a reflection on the crew!

Burnley & Pendle named their minibus operation 'Whizzard' giving them the prize for the most tenuous name by local association. At one point in 1988 B&P, incredibly, had a GMPTE contract to provide weekend operation of the Manchester Centreline service, which is why 87 was to be found outside the city's Royal Exchange.

GM Standards really did pop up everywhere after deregulation, and 43 here was one of eleven Greater Manchester Fleetlines to move north. It looked rather smart in its new livery and Rossendale got five years' work from it.

Brand-new full size buses were hard to find in the late 1980s – the market was too volatile, too uncertain. But Burnley & Pendle found the confidence to buy both single deckers and double deckers including ten Volvo Citybuses including 109, seen at Burnley bus station.

Blackburn – and deregulation in a nutshell. Blackburn, Ribble, Hyndburn and Ribble minibuses all fight for passengers. Those who had once co-operated now had to fight. It was all very sad and although it was exciting, at the same time it was clear that the old times had gone for ever.

Lancaster City Transport found itself in a life-and-death struggle with Ribble. Ex-Bournemouth Atlantean 245 was one of a fleet of drafted-in buses but although Lancaster saw out the end of the eighties, by 1992 it was all over and Stagecoach emerged as the victor.

Yet another GM Standard? No, take a close look – it's a late Atlantean with the 'alloy' Northern Counties body. This had been Barrow 107; in 1989 Barrow gave up the unequal struggle and were bought by their main competitor. 107 was new in 1984 but wasn't taxed after 1991 – a very short life for a good bus.

Hyndburn 194 looks a little hemmed-in, and no wonder – Accrington seemed to attract more than its fair share of 'pirate' operators after 1986. CUF261L had been new to Southdown and YCH898M was new to Trent but they were now working for Accrington Coachways.

Blackburn expanded its coaching operations using a series of good second-hand purchases including 307, which had started life with National Travel (East). It looked like a nice day in Accrington, and a smooth and speedy ride on a Leopard sounds very enticing.

Cumbria

Rural Cumbria might be expected to be a backwater in bus terms, but that would be unfair. In 1980 it was the home of NBC subsidiary Cumberland Motor Services in the west; yet further patches of Ribble territory in the south, east, and the north around Carlisle; and just one municipal operator, Barrow Corporation Transport.

Cumberland Motor Services, based in Whitehaven, was once a Tilling operator and in 1980 its fleet still contained plenty of its Bristol/ECW heritage, but it also had plenty of Leyland Nationals too – not a surprise as the Leyland National factory was in Lillyhall, in the middle of Cumberland territory. This provided useful works traffic but the lifeblood of Cumberland Motor Services, and the foundation of the company's prosperity, was the giant complex at Sellafield south of Egremont. CMS had an effectively monopoly on services serving the huge plant, which was big enough to support an internal bus service around the site for workers, and every morning and evening poppy red buses would fill the roads between Sellafield and Millom, Whitehaven, or Frizington. The use of so many buses just for shift changes can't have been economic but it was work, and the operators of Sellafield were known to pay top dollar for, well, just about anything.

Ribble was dominant in a wide arc surrounding Cumberland territory, with incursions from the south via the border with Lancashire; then stretching in a corridor along the M6 and A6 taking in Kendal, Keswick and Penrith; and finally a network around Carlisle, home to Ribble services since the 1920s but augmented in early NBC days via a swap with United Auto. Ribble's Cumbrian network had once crawled spider-like along almost every A-road and B-road in its area, but the economics of such services had always been shaky and by the 1970s was totally unsustainable. However, the company's Leopards were still liable to appear round the corner of many a Lakeland road.

Barrow Corporation ploughed its own furrow, running local services close to the town and leaving inter-urban links to the big red neighbour. Up the coast towards Workington might seem to be very sparse territory and such it was, but even so Whitehaven was the cradle of deregulation when local Yeowart's managed – in the teeth of opposition from Cumberland – to create a network of town services in direct competition to the established operator. It was a portent of things to come.

At first sight, the advent of deregulation didn't bring the day one transformation seen in the bigger towns and cities further south. Barrow and Ribble fought for supremacy in south-west Furness: there could be only one winner and Barrow capitulated, collapsing with its remains sold to the 'aggressor' in 1989. Ribble and Cumberland found themselves both part of the Stagecoach group not long after the break-up of NBC so they didn't so much compete as straighten lines, so that Cumberland effectively took over Ribble's operations north of Morecambe Bay. Cumberland had bought out the troublesome Yeowart's of Whitehaven, so apart from around Barrow, Cumbria looked similar in 1990 to 1980; with Stagecoach stripes in abundance, fewer villages served, and no more real choice than before deregulation.

Cumbria, apart from west Cumbria, was Ribble territory. From the late 1960s to the early 1980s it was criss-crossed by these pretty Leopards, nicknamed 'Red Setters'. 527 was photographed at Ulverston depot and looks like it had been on a trip to Ambleside.

There were some places that not even Ribble ventured, and Mountain Goat of Bowness took up the slack running minibuses – and a Bedford OB – over the hills and far away. Ford Transit AVR312M was photographed at Wasdale Head Inn on the 'Wasdale Flyer' service, possibly England's most remote bus terminus.

Barrow was historically a Lancashire municipal, having been part of 'Lancashire over the sands', and in the early 1980s had a traditional deep blue and cream livery. The fleet was mainly single deckers with an assortment of Leopards, single deck Fleetlines and Nationals as shown by 17 at the depot.

Carlisle was Ribble's most Northern outpost but it housed the usual company assortment of REs, Nationals, Atlanteans, and VRs. 333 was based in Cumbria for a long time and ended its days at Carlisle until withdrawn in 1985.

Even after the M6 came, Anglo-Scottish services could often be found passing through Carlisle's bus station. Almost-new Western Scottish's V128 made an impressive sight in October 1982 although its Duple body didn't quite capture the elegance of the Alexander M-type original.

Cumberland ran into Carlisle from the Maryport direction, and Bristol VR 431 was standard fare for the long run to Whitehaven. 431 lasted a long time in service, until 2006, and then entered preservation. No white stripe at the front means this is the ultra-low height version, just 13 feet 5 inches tall.

Back in 1969 Ribble and United had done a 'tidying up' that gave Ribble all United's Carlisle services including the long 685 to Newcastle, where 1012 was found resting in 1984. There were just ten of these Bristol RE/ECW coaches and they made for a lovely tuneful ride along the long A69 road.

Wrights Brothers of Nenthead ran – and in 2017, still run – a Keswick – Newcastle service via Alston. Surprisingly for such an arduous trip they preferred Bedfords, and SAO466X looked immaculate when seen at Newcastle Marlborough Crecent, about to return home.

Ribble moved seamlessly from the National 1 to the National 2 – a very good bus that had all the good parts of the National (the body structure) without its main drawback (the 500-series engine). 882 would make some splendid sound effects on its journey from Carlisle to Penrith.

Barrow Corporation bought Northern Counties-bodied Atlanteans with the Greater Manchester style of 'alloy body', and very smart they looked too. 104 was resting at the depot in July 1986.

Sellafield was Cumberland's big industrial traffic source – several times a day to coincide with shift changes, Sellafield's bus station would be the start or end point for works services from far afield. These three Nationals, built just up the road at Lillyhall, will soon be busy.

Ribble had a small outstation at Appleby-in-Westmorland, based at an old goods shed next to the railway station. 1113 was very comfortable for long rural journeys, but its four steps to the saloon was less than ideal. Even so, it spent its entire career in Cumbria.

Barrow Corporation didn't wait for deregulation to get its ration of DMSs – it bought three in 1982 and gave them this attractive livery. The surroundings are less attractive – it's Ramsden Dock and 103 was being used in connection with an open day at the BNFL sea terminal.

In October 1986, this was a common scene outside many a bus garage – redundant buses not needed in the new deregulated world. Barrow's elderly scrappers here consisted of two Leopards (49 and 57) and two unusual single deck Fleetlines, 1 and 2.

In a prototype for the later 1986 deregulation, Yeowart's of Whitehaven was allowed to compete with local incumbent Cumberland. The fight was nothing short of brutal and ended with Cumberland buying the insurgent and painting some buses in Yeowart livery for a while.

Cumberland's NBC identity was still intact in March 1988 when ex-Trent 606 was captured passing Seker's fabrics mill in Moresby Road, Whitehaven. Comfy for a town service, but not a good prospect for baby buggies.

At deregulation Barrow Corporation rebranded as 'BBT' – Barrow Borough Transport. 1968-built 62 was a pretty ancient survivor considering GMT was selling off Standards ten years younger, but it soldiered on until 1988 before being scrapped.

Ribble's Carlisle operations passed to Cumberland in 1986 and for a time were branded 'CarlisleBus'. Here's the inevitable DMS doing duty in English Street, long since pedestrianised.

Western Scottish were still to be seen in Carlisle after 1986 but there was no attempt to move en masse across the border. DS559 was a Seddon Pennine based in Dumfries, but was parked in Carlisle's bus station parking area when photographed.

Ribble's coach Olympians made a fine sight when clean. In May 1988 2179 was on rail replacement duties outside Carlisle station as the line to Maryport was closed, and would probably give a more comfortable ride than the BR Class 108 DMUs still in use on that line.

British Nuclear Fuels plc created a new Sellafield Visitor Centre in 1987, and two futuristic Duple 425 integrals were bought for tours of the main site. D361VHH was photographed at Duple's Blackpool factory on completion. They were quite superb vehicles.

Barrow brightened up its blue colour scheme for deregulation, and Leyland National 10 looked quite smart as it approached the town along Abbey Road.

Freed from NBC corporate identity, Cumberland rebranded as 'cms' for 'Cumberland Motor Services'. A new and rather attractive red, cream and brown livery was adopted and Carlislebus 40 wore it well when seen in Carlisle's Bank Street.

For a short period Cumberland's Carlislebus operation operated under NBC auspices, so ex-Ribble 1477 marked a hybrid stage. It was a late survivor in this style – when photographed in May 1989, most of the fleet was in the new cms red and cream scheme.

Cumberland 633 had been delivered in 1981 in full National Express white, but by April 1988 it was a in a 'Border Clipper' scheme and either fresh from, or about to embark on, a run a Silloth – a pretty but isolated town on the Solway Firth.

Carlisle had its ration of Routemasters: 904 had once been London Transport RM1933 and I photographed it in 'LT50' livery at Chiswick in 1983. So it was a surprise to find it again in English Street in 1989, and an even bigger surprise when I saw it again in London in 2012.

We saw Barrow Corporation 104 a few pages ago in traditional Barrow livery – here it is again in post-deregulation BBT livery, waiting in Duke Street outside the town hall. The Hawcoat route was just two miles long and doesn't look busy in this photo.

Cumberland had a surprisingly small proportion of full coaches for an operator covering the Western Lakes, but 633 was delivered in white for the company's contributions to National Express services. It looked better in cms red in Carlisle bus station, on a service to Penrith.

So the new age dawned, with Stagecoach buying Cumberland and applying corporate stripes to everything. 1003 was one of the first buses for Cumberland bought new by Stagecoach, and was an Olympian with eighty-seven seats in its Alexander body. The location is Carlisle's Botchergate, close to the railway station.

Acknowledgements

This book was compiled using my own photographs from the time as the starting point: but my travels still left many, many gaps and I am truly indebted to my good friend of over thirty years' standing, David Stubbins, for supplying many images. There were still some photos needed and I am very grateful to Glen Bubb, Warren Vipond, Chris Wilcock, and Mark Youdan for their contributions.

All author's and photographers' royalties have been donated to the Greater Manchester Transport Society. The Museum is in Boyle Street, Manchester M8 8UW, and contains around eighty local buses as well as photographs, documents, and other artefacts that tell the story of public road transport in Greater Manchester. See www.gmts.co.uk for details.

This book is dedicated to my children Heather and Adam, of whom I am very proud.